THE
WISDEN
BOOK OF
CRICKET HERO

BATSMEN

THE
WISDEN
BOOK OF
CRICKET HEROES

BATSMEN

ALAN LEE

Stanley Paul
London Sydney Auckland Johannesburg

Stanley Paul & Co. Ltd

An imprint of Century Hutchinson Ltd

62–65 Chandos Place, London WC2N 4NW

Century Hutchinson Australia (Pty) Ltd
89–91 Albion Street, Surry Hills, NSW 2010

Century Hutchinson New Zealand Limited
PO Box 40–086, Glenfield, Auckland 10

Century Hutchinson South Africa (Pty) Ltd
PO Box 337, Bergvlei 2012, South Africa

First published 1989
Reprinted 1989 (twice)
© Alan Lee 1989

Set in 11/13pt Plantin by Input Typesetting Ltd., London

Printed & Bound in Great Britain by Mackays of Chatham PLC, Letchworth.

British Library Cataloguing in Publication Data

Lee, Alan, *1954*
    The Wisden book of cricket heroes: Batsmen
    1. Cricket. Biographies. Collections
    I. Title
    796.35'8'0922
ISBN 0 09 173835 0

CONTENTS

Acknowledgement

The author and publishers would like to thank Adrian Murrell of All-Sport UK Ltd, who supplied all the photographs.

Introduction

Every cricket follower, no matter his age, fancies himself as a selector. Some may be more dogmatic than others, some more realistic, but I doubt if there is a single fan of our summer game who has not, at some time, indulged himself in picking an England team to beat the choice of the selectors, or a world team to beat the West Indies.

The great attraction is that the possibilities are endless and the responsibility nil. No-one is ever going to disprove your argument that a certain batting order is very much better than the one being persevered with by the official selectors; no-one is going to pit your World XI against Mars and show they are eminently beatable. Picking teams creates a theatre for healthy debate.

As a boy, I was forever frittering away time which ought to have been spent on school homework in the idle pursuit of choosing my own favourite England side, or a World side of left-handers, etc. I am lucky. The job I have now entitles me to go on record with my version of an England team before every Test Match. If the selectors' choices differ, I can criticize – but it is still their team which has to go out and be judged.

I jumped at the chance to select my own batting and bowling heroes for these two Wisden books. Wouldn't anyone? But when I actually sat down to condense the candidates to twenty, for each category, I began to experience the problems of the real selector. There were so many options, so many difficult decisions.

No doubt my choices will not meet with universal approval. I have omitted players reluctantly, included others tentatively. My only provisos were that everyone involved should have played Test cricket (in the case of Graeme Pollock, unofficial Tests) during the 1980s.

Now that I have made my choices and, in the pages which follow, sought to justify them, I have only one regret. I wish I could form some of these players into my own, Sunday afternoon team . . . now, that is a fantasy world.

ALLAN BORDER

RECORD

Allan Robert Border was born in the Sydney suburb of Cremorne on 27 July 1955. A left-handed batsman and occasional slow left-arm bowler, he was already 21 years old when he first played for New South Wales. In 1980 he transferred his home and allegiance to Queensland, whom he has captained since 1983. Border made his Test debut for Australia in the 1978–9 series against England and has since played more than 100 Test Matches. He has been captain of his country since November, 1984, and has also played more limited-overs internationals than anyone in the world. The highest score of his career is the 196 scored in the Lord's Test of 1985; seven of his Test centuries have been against England. He has also played two seasons of county cricket for Essex.

‘ He sells his wicket so dearly as to drive a bowler to dismay ’

TECHNIQUE

There are certain batsmen who can inspire awe and admiration through their power or elegance, who can send the spectator away with golden memories of an innings worth no more than 20 or 30. Then there are others, like Allan Border, whose great assets are pugnacity, determination and courage. They may not excite the casual onlooker but they produce consistent results and win the lasting respect of their team-mates.

In the course of ten years as an international player, Border has established himself as one of the top five batsmen in the world. He may not have the arrogant majesty of Vivian Richards but, whatever the game, whatever the context, he sells his wicket so dearly as to drive a bowler to despair. If you had to choose a man to bat for your life, Border's qualities would be irresistible.

Footwork and shot selection are the keys to his great success. In his early years he was considered susceptible against fast bowlers attacking him around off stump but the years have brought mature judgement to his game. He has always been an adroit player of the short ball, pulling and cutting ferociously, and one of his trademarks is to emerge from periods of introspective defence with a booming cover-drive. His concentration is intense and inexhaustible, his will to win is something to behold and to imitate.

HIGHLIGHTS 🏆

Cricket could easily have lost Allan Border to its American sister sport, baseball. It could also have lost him to the beach. As a young man in sun-kissed Sydney, these were the passions which jostled for his attention. Oddly, it was an Englishman, former Test cricketer Barry Knight, who persuaded him that he had a big future in the game if only he would work at it. Border has never forgotten the advice. He graduated through the New South Wales colts team, into the state side and then, when Australia lost many stars to Kerry Packer's World Series Cricket circuit, he received his Test call-up.

If there were rough edges to his game in those early days, the desire to succeed was as obvious as it is today. Two contrasting incidents, within a year of his Test debut, illustrate the point. In December of 1979, with England visiting Australia for the second successive winter, Border felt his place in the side under pressure through the return of the Packer players. The First Test was at Perth and Border, batting number three, was rapidly lbw to Ian Botham for only four. Feeling furious, with himself as much as the decision, he strode off the pitch into the sanctuary of the dressing-room, where he threw down his bat, kicked away his gloves and verbally gave vent to his emotions . . . only to discover his awful blunder – he was in England's dressing-room! Suitably embarrassed, another lesson digested, he went out in the second innings to make a marvellous, match-winning century.

Three months later, in the final Test of a gruelling winter, he became the only man in history to score 150 in each innings of a Test Match, achieving the feat against Pakistan in Lahore. By then, one assumes, he felt confident of his place in the team, but his doughty, gutsy professionalism has never faltered to this day. He is intensely patriotic and considers an Australian defeat to be a personal insult. It is this commitment which helps make him the great player he is.

On a turning pitch, the sweep is the batsman's constant stand-by. Here, Border shows the value of getting low to play the shot, picking the length and rotating the trunk of the body

Ian Botham

Record 📖

Ian Terence Botham was born in Heswall, Cheshire on 24 November 1955. A right-handed, middle-order batsman, powerfully built, he made his debut for Somerset in 1974, while still a teenager. He played for the county until 1986, including two years as captain, before transferring to Worcestershire. He first played for England in 1977, against Australia and has now scored more than 5,000 runs, including 14 centuries, in 94 Test Match appearances, 12 of them as captain. He has made nine full England tours but his most remarkable deeds have been performed on home territory, including a score of 208 against India, in 1982, and two superb centuries against Australia in 1981. In 1985 he created a new record by hitting 80 sixes in the English first-class season.

❛He is the greatest match-winner the game has ever known❜

Mike Brearley, 1985

Technique 🏏

The mere mention of Ian Botham conjures an impression of adventure and heroism, of uninhibited attack. Quite right, too. Botham has played innumerable innings of extraordinary aggression and would doubtless like to be remembered that way. He is, however, very far from being simply a slogger. His technique, if not his temperament, would fill all the requirements of an opening batsman. There are those, indeed, who consider that he is the most technically correct of all current England batsmen.

From a classically sideways-on stance, he plays with a high, flourishing backlift, but brings the bat down ramrod straight. His footwork is positive and nimble, his range of strokes often quite breathtaking. When he does fail, it is frequently through impatience or impetuosity rather than any forced error. Botham is a man who believes the ball is for hitting and, although he has played with discipline and restraint for England when circumstances have demanded, defence is basically foreign to his nature.

The most vividly recalled of Botham's shots are the booming straight drive, completed with an extravagant follow-through, and the savage carve through the off-side off the back foot. Power is not everything to him, though, and he can late cut or leg-glance, sweep and controversially reverse sweep, with equal facility and transparent relish.

HIGHLIGHTS 🏆

Nothing went right for Ian Botham during the first half of 1981. Of all the turbulent times in his frantically full life, this was the most depressing. He began the year as England captain in the West Indies, on a tour fraught with problems both on and off the field. England were well beaten and the team dramatically left Guyana after one player, Robin Jackman, had been issued with a deportation order. Worse still, Ken Barrington, the team's assistant manager and a trusted friend and adviser to Botham, died of a heart attack. It was the worst of times and, back home to begin the new season, Botham's personal fortunes nosedived still further. The first Test against Australia was lost; then, in a draw at Lord's, Botham made nought in each innings. Dejected and distraught, his customary buoyancy and humour damaged beyond belief, he resigned the captaincy, only to discover that the selectors had already decided to sack him.

He stayed in the team, of course, and with Mike Brearley resuming the leadership, an astonishing transformation overtook both his own and England's form. The Third Test at Headingley was one of the most sensational ever played and it firmly restored Botham as one of the game's great folk heroes.

It appeared to be heading remorselessly towards an Australian win when England, obliged to follow-on, collapsed again. Botham came in at a desperate 105 for five. Soon, it was still worse – England 92 runs adrift and with only three wickets standing. It was mid-afternoon on the fourth day; England's players, abandoning hope of salvation, had by now checked out of their hotel and Ladbrokes were offering 500–1 against an England win. These are the type of odds Botham has always loved – the challenge of the wildly unlikely. In the next three hours he turned the game and, as it transpired, the series. Destroying the bowling of Lillee and Alderman, which had caused England such torment, he rushed to 145 not out with a series of spectacular drives and pulls. He earned a lead of 129 and history relates that Bob Willis completed mission impossible with the best bowling of his life. England went on to win the next two Tests through further heroics from a revitalised Botham. It was the greatest summer of his career, hard on the heels of the most miserable winter and spring. He was uncontainable, irrepressible, a superman to bring a smile to the nation. Few cricketers have ever given so much pleasure.

GEOFF BOYCOTT

RECORD 📖

Geoffrey Boycott was born in the Yorkshire mining village of Fitzwilliam on 21 October 1940. After a grammar school education he made his debut for Yorkshire in 1962 and was capped a year later. In 1964, he made the first of 108 Test appearances for England, stretching over 18 years. He was captain of Yorkshire from 1971 to 1978 and also captained England four times. A right-handed, opening batsman, he made 1,000 runs in 23 consecutive domestic seasons and, in 1971, he aggregated 2,503. In all, he made 151 centuries, of which 22 were in Test Matches, his highest score for England being 246 not out against India, at Leeds in 1967. He retired at the end of the 1986 season but remained active on Yorkshire's committee.

❛ I play best when I'm surrounded by people who appreciate me ❜

Boycott, 1980

TECHNIQUE 🏏

Many batsmen have been born with more natural flair than Geoff Boycott but few have made greater use of their resources. By extraordinary diligence and single-minded ambition, Boycott literally manufactured the player he wanted to be, the cornerstone of England's batting, the man whose wicket was sold more dearly than, perhaps, that of anyone in contemporary world cricket. He was utterly self-made and justly proud of it.

His critics, of whom he has seldom been short, will say that Boycott's game was based on selfish principles, that he all too frequently promoted his own interests and aims above those of his team. Boycott himself will dismiss this as the jealous reaction of those who envy his success and cannot understand his motivation. There have been times, however, when slow scoring has been his downfall, never more sensationally so than in 1967, when the England selectors' response to his career-best score of 246 not out was to drop him from the next Test Match.

This is not to say he was incapable of fast scoring. Any who witnessed the 1965 Gillette Cup final will be familiar with his vast array of strokes. He dominated that day, scoring 146 in Yorkshire's massive victory over Surrey and astonishing those who had already dismissed him as boring and strokeless. He has seldom recaptured the mood, instead carving a formidable reputation as a defensive master who has eliminated risks and shortcomings simply by dropping shots which got him out too often. He is a classical straight and cover-driver, a poised master of the on-drive and a resourceful accumulator through the on-side. His most vivid epitaph, though, will be the impregnable forward defensive shot, tormentor of so many bowlers down the years.

HIGHLIGHTS

Geoff Boycott was a man of consuming ambitions at the crease, a player who set himself stiff targets and then microscopically examined any failure to achieve them. One such target was the milestone of 100 first-class centuries, previously attained by only two Yorkshiremen, Herbert Sutcliffe and Len Hutton. Both are cricketing legends and Boycott yearned to be regarded in the same bracket. By the way he reached this particular target, however, he may even have exceeded his own lofty anticipation.

On 11 August 1977, Boycott became the first man ever to score his hundredth century in a Test Match. Better still, it was a Test against Australia and, the rich icing on the cake, it was in front of his own adoring fans at Headingley, Leeds. If he had written the script himself, Boycott might even have feared he was being greedy.

The Yorkshire public, confident of seeing history enacted, were shoehorned into the ground, the gates being closed well before the start. Their conviction was based on solid ground for, a fortnight earlier, Boycott had returned from three years of self-imposed Test exile to score 107 and 80 not out in the victorious Third Test, batting on all five days of the game. Now England, 2–0 up in the series, needed only a draw to regain the Ashes. Boycott ensured they did very much better than that. He did so in his own, time-honoured way, never hurrying despite the apparent tension of the occasion. He scored only 34 by lunch, a further 35 by tea. Finally, after five hours and 20 minutes of intense concentration, he on-drove Greg Chappell for four to the accompaniment of a deafening roar from the ecstatically relieved crowd. Boycott an emotional and sensitive man beneath his calculating, steely veneer, pumped the air with his arms and seemed, briefly, lost in the triumph of the moment. Who can blame him? 'Somehow,' he later wrote, 'I was destined to get a century that day . . . this was the most magical moment of my life.'

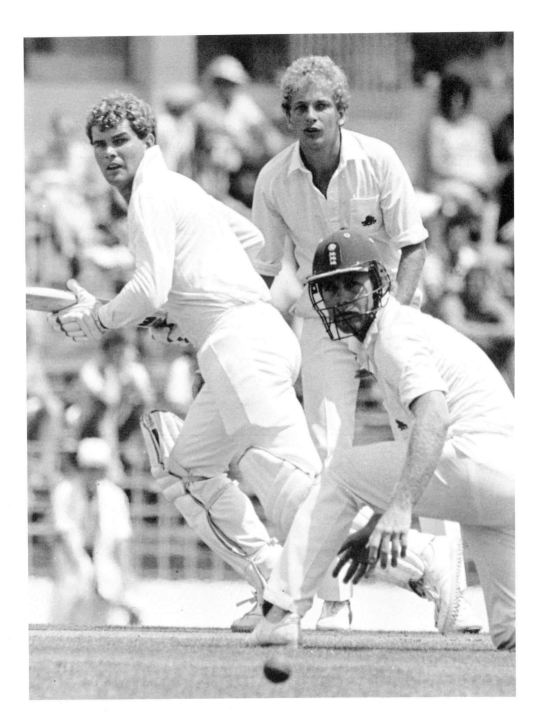

MARTIN CROWE

RECORD 📖

Martin David Crowe was born in Henderson, Auckland, on 22 September 1962. A right-handed batsman and, until injury intervened, a medium-pace bowler, he is the son of David Crowe, who played provincial cricket in New Zealand, and the younger brother of Jeff, a New Zealand batsman and captain. Tall, fair-haired and stockily built, Crowe first played for Auckland at the age of 17 and made his Test debut two years later. He spent a season with Somerset in 1984 and returned to them in 1987, the year in which he scored 4,045 in all first-class cricket. A batsman of grace and elegance, he has now developed into one of the finest players ever to come out of New Zealand and can be regarded among the top five batsmen in the world today.

❛He gives a bowler the impression he might as well go home❜

TECHNIQUE 🏏

Here is an example of a player who grew immeasurably in stature as a result of experiencing county cricket. Not in technique or stroke play – Martin Crowe was already intimidatingly good in such areas – but in attitude and aptitude. After the 1984 season, in which he achieved the considerable feat of successfully deputising for Viv Richards at Taunton,

Crowe said he had learned more in six months than he had done in the preceding six years. He emerged from the tutorial a better, more complete cricketer and New Zealand were the beneficiaries.

There are ways in which Crowe resembles Geoffrey Boycott. He is similarly self-critical, analysing his dismissals and his failings with unsparing intensity. He can also be introspective, sometimes appearing difficult or uncommunicative – this, despite the evidence of his first year at Somerset, where his concern for the younger players extended to setting up a club for the uncapped men on the staff. He is, anyway, at his most expressive when batting at times when he feels fortune and form are running high. Then, he gives a bowler the impression he might

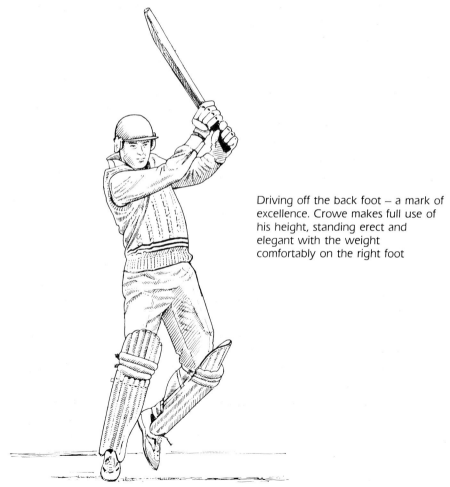

Driving off the back foot – a mark of excellence. Crowe makes full use of his height, standing erect and elegant with the weight comfortably on the right foot

as well go home. His technique is immaculate, flawlessly correct in defence and attractive yet textbook in attack. Again, like Boycott, he scorns unnecessary risks, yet his range of shots is such that he can dominate an attack without appearing to hurry.

HIGHLIGHTS 🏆

For far too long, New Zealand lived in the cricketing shadows of Australia. They were visited, by lofty rivals, only as an afterthought to a full tour of Australia and it was not until the mid-1970s that their neighbours even condescended to provide regular opposition. It is, then, easily understood that their first victory in a series over Australia was cause for national rejoicing. At the centre of the triumph were two outstanding cricketers: one was Richard Hadlee, whose bowling was on a different plane from anyone else, and the other was Martin Crowe.

It was in November of 1985 that the unthinkable began to happen to proud Australia – defeat in their own back yard by their upstart cousins from across the Tasman Sea. At Brisbane, in the First Test, Australia were humbled by Hadlee's bowling – he took nine for 52 and six for 71 – and tormented by Crowe's flowering talent as a batsman. At 85 for two, Crowe joined John Reid in a stand ultimately worth 224, a New Zealand third-wicket record. On and on went Crowe, equalling his highest Test score of 188 and setting up a declaration with a huge lead of 374. Despite a brave century from the Australian captain, Allan Border, it was enough to give New Zealand victory by an innings.

The Second Test, at Sydney, was lost by four wickets but, regrouping with a resolve which many had considered beyond them, New Zealand won the final Test by six wickets to take the series 2–1. By now the public attention, initially elsewhere, had been riveted by the struggle – the Third Test, on the Perth ground, drew three times as many spectators as the First. Those who came saw Hadlee take another 11 wickets and Crowe, inspired by the prospect of making history, score 71 and 42 not out, every run a hard-fought triumph on a suspect pitch where neither side managed a score of 300. He was there at the end, steering New Zealand to their most momentous win with just ten overs to spare. Three months later, back on home soil in Christchurch, Crowe took another 137 off Australia – and New Zealand, instilled with a new self-confidence in their cricketing ability, went on to win that series, too.

MIKE GATTING

RECORD 📖

Michael William Gatting was born in Kingsbury, Middlesex on 6 June 1957. A right-handed batsman and medium-pace bowler, he established a big reputation in schools and club cricket before making his debut for Middlesex at the age of 18. He received his county cap in 1977 and made his first England appearance later the same year, in Pakistan. He was to suffer many disappointments at Test level before securing an unchallenged place in the England side on the tour of India in 1984–5. In June of 1986 he was appointed England captain; on his first tour in charge, the Ashes were won. He was dismissed as captain precisely two years after taking the job, but his batting retained its quality throughout his troubles.

'He went to India believing he was on a last chance; he came back as a hero'

TECHNIQUE 🏏

To his many admirers, the enigma of Mike Gatting's career is that it took so long to reach the heights of which he was so obviously capable. Year after year, Gatting would amass closer to 2,000 than 1,000 runs for Middlesex, frequently treating the best of county attacks with contempt. Yet, each time he put on an England sweater, it was as if he adopted a different, less impressive identity. Composure and command were replaced by diffidence, not to mention a penchant for basic errors of judgement. What he lacked was confidence and when that arrived, transmitted by the faith shown in him by the then England captain David Gower, he was a different proposition. Suddenly, he was doing for England what he had always done for Middlesex, backing his ability against the best and worst of bowling, constantly taking the attack to the opposition. In no time at all, he made the transition from frustrated fringe player to established front-line star.

Gatting's major strength was also once seen as his great weakness: he plays all the shots. If there have been times when he has lost his wicket by playing too freely, however, there have been many more, especially in recent years, when he has influenced the result of a match by his refusal to allow good bowling to sedate his stroke-play. Predominantly a powerful, back-foot player, specialising in the square-cut and the pull, he is also never afraid to hit the ball in the air and is a renowned destroyer of slow bowling.

HIGHLIGHTS ♟

For all the conflicting emotions, the absurdly contrasting peaks and troughs of his two-year spell as England captain, Mike Gatting will probably look back upon the winter of 1984–5 as the most influential, and the most pleasurable of his life. He went to India believing he was on a last chance; he came back as a hero.

It had been a very long road to Shangri-la for the boy from north London, born into a sporting family and with a natural love of both cricket and football. His brother, Steve, chose to play football and went on to play in the FA Cup Final for Brighton. Mike, having played football at junior level for Watford, opted for cricket as a career. He had scored his first century at the age of 11, and a stunning innings it was – he made 102 not out, of a winning total of 115 for eight, for Wykeham Juniors. He was talent-spotted by Middlesex at the age of 15 and things never stopped happening for him until he reached the dizzy heights of Test cricket. Then, it was as if he was treading water.

By the time he went out to bat against India, at Bombay in late November 1984, Gatting had played 54 Test innings for England over a period of seven years. He had not scored a single century and his average was in the low twenties. There were those who thought the selectors were mad to persistently turn back to him. But, with England facing a first-innings deficit of 270, and already struggling in their second, Gatting at last came good with an innings of 136. England still lost the match but it was, as he freely admits, the turning point of a career which was threatening to lose its way. Tucked away in his cricket bag, Gatting had two lucky charms – parting gifts from his wife and son. They now travel with him wherever he goes, and who can wonder? Later in that same series, Gatting scored 207 in the Madras Test, still his highest score for England. Since Bombay, however, the centuries have come regularly and, despite his voluntary exile from the England side after losing the captaincy in 1988, Gatting remains an enduring star of the eighties.

SUNIL GAVASKAR

RECORD 📖

Sunil Manohar Gavaskar was born in Bombay, India on 10 July 1949. A right-handed, opening batsman and very occasional medium-pace bowler, he retired from first-class cricket in late 1987, holding a mass of batting records. He has played more Tests, scored more runs and made more centuries and half-centuries than anyone in the history of international cricket. His tally of 10,122 runs is more than 2,000 superior to anyone else and, through his 17-year Test career, he maintained a remarkable average of more than 50. His prolific deeds began in his debut Test series, back in 1971, when in four Tests against the West Indies, he amassed 774 runs. In all, he scored 17 of his 34 Test hundreds against the West Indies. He captained his country 40 times and is the only Indian captain to have won more Tests than he lost.

'A masterful player of fast bowling through his exceptional balance and judgement'

TECHNIQUE 🏏

If one had to describe Sunny Gavaskar's batting in a single word, then 'patience' would fit the bill. In the calculating fashion of Geoff Boycott and Glenn Turner, he could sometimes be thought boring, such was his attention to the details of defence and survival, but in the later stages of his career he allowed his foot to depress the accelerator pedal rather more often, without ever sacrificing his technique to slog.

A short man, only 5 feet 5 inches, Gavaskar has honed a method to suit his stature. A masterful player of fast bowling through his exceptional balance and judgement, he would defend solidly for over after nagging over yet still have accumulated steady runs by brilliant placement of the ball and, a neglected but important art, skilful poaching of the quick single. The best players know instinctively where every fielder is placed and will react to their own shot into space with the speed which produces a run when for many mortals it would not exist.

The merit of Gavaskar's astonishing record is reinforced by the situations in which he was often forced to bat. For much of his career, India were not a strong batting side, tending to rely heavily on 'The Little Master' and his brother-in-law, the similarly tiny Viswanath. If they failed, the pack of cards would collapse. Moreover, Gavaskar had to bear the brunt of some uninhibited intimidation from opposition fast bowlers for the simple fact that India had none of their own with whom to retaliate. His consistency against such odds marks him down as one of the finest players the world has seen, a model for any aspiring youngster.

HIGHLIGHTS 🏆

Asking Sunil Gavaskar to name his greatest innings is akin to asking Jimmy Greaves to nominate his best goal, or Lester Piggott his finest race. There are so many in the selection that the choice is inevitably swayed by the mood of the moment. Gavaskar's personal choice, from his 214 Test Match innings, goes back to 1974 at Old Trafford. It was a pitch ideal for seam and swing bowling; England, with Willis, Old and Hendrick, were ideally equipped. Out of an Indian total of 246, Gavaskar contributed 101, his first century against England, a triumph of technique and application. The match was lost but, in this country, a reputation was made.

To most Englishmen, however, the outstanding memory of Gavaskar might come from slightly more recent times – from 1979, or even from 1987. On the first occasion, it was the final Test of a four-match series, played at The Oval. England, already 1–0 up, needed only a draw to take the rubber and that much seemed certain when they set an apparently impossible target of 438 runs in the final four sessions of the game. Gavaskar, who had temporarily lost the Indian captaincy for this series, responded with a monumental innings of 221, his 20th Test century and then his highest score. As the hours eked away and the runs piled up, the unthinkable became conceivable. With just eight overs left, India were only 49 runs short of an incredible win, seven wickets still intact. Then, at last, it was over, Gower catching Gavaskar off Botham. In the frantic final overs, India lost their way, ending nine runs adrift with two wickets left after one of the greatest ever Tests.

Nine years on, and back in London again, Gavaskar filled a strange vacancy in his cluttered career with his first century at Lord's. It came in the glittering MCC Bicentenary Match and, typically, he extended it to a massive 188. When he was out, only just failing to mark the occasion with a double-century of his own, the ground stood to give him an emotional farewell. The previous evening, 'Sunny' had announced that this would be his last first-class match. What a way to go!

Graham Gooch

Record 📖

Graham Alan Gooch was born at Leytonstone, Essex on 23 July 1953. A right-handed batsman and medium-pace swing bowler, he first played for Essex in 1973 and was selected for England two years later, when only 21. Although this was a false dawn to his Test career, he was always destined for great things and would have been an England regular throughout the eighties but for serving a three-year Test suspension in the wake of the unsanctioned South African tour of 1982. He has, since the retirement of Geoff Boycott, been unquestionably the finest opening batsman in England. In 1988, after playing outstandingly well against the rampant West Indies, he was appointed as England captain.

❛ Gooch seemed to face hopeless odds, but you would never have known it ❜

Wisden on his 1979 century v. West Indies

Technique 🏏

In the later years of his prolific batting career, Graham Gooch has undergone an identity change. No longer is he the carefree assassin of bowling, the belligerent frontman who will live and die by the sword. In the fashion of a personality discarding the cavalier outlook of youth for the responsibilities of adult life, Gooch has adapted his batting to the burden of seniority. Often, at county and international level, he has felt obliged to play the part of anchor-man for fear of collapse if he should depart early; if this is an admirable reaction by the best player in the side, it is also rather sad that we see fewer of the dashing, attacking innings which were once his forte.

More than once, over the years, Gooch has suffered periods of intense self-doubt, when form and confidence have deserted him and he has questioned whether they will ever return. A very diligent and thorough professional, his response has invariably been to examine his own technique for flaws, studying and re-studying video-tapes of his recent innings and comparing them with the past.

He bats now with the exaggerated, raised bat stance, but it suits him well. He is a masterly player of fast bowling, his studied back-foot

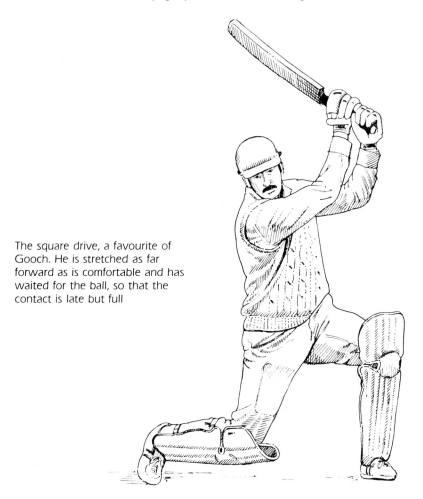

The square drive, a favourite of Gooch. He is stretched as far forward as is comfortable and has waited for the ball, so that the contact is late but full

defence giving way to the occasional crashing straight drive or square cut when the bowler's length wavers. He will still destroy poor bowling; he will survive and prosper against the best.

HIGHLIGHTS 🏆

The 1980 West Indians in England won their Test series by only 1–0, a far cry from the 5–0 and 4–0 beatings handed out by their merciless successors in 1984 and 1988. As a team, however, they suffered little by comparison and their fast bowling attack was arguably at its absolute peak. Only once, in the course of the series, did an English batsman genuinely dominate. It happened on a grey June day at Lord's when Gooch scored his first Test century, in his 36th innings.

The opposition attack was led by Andy Roberts and Michael Holding. The back-up came from Joel Garner and Colin Croft. Boycott, the lynchpin of the side, was out early to Holding. The innings was interrupted by bad light. Gooch seemed to face hopeless odds but you would never have known it. The *Wisden Almanack* of 1981 recalled that 'Gooch played with an authority and power seldom seen from an Englishman in the last 15 years or so.' Driving and hooking mightily, he scored 123 out of 165 in only three and a half hours. Those who were there still speak of the innings today, for it was a day of magic, best summarised by the fact that a century by Viv Richards, the following day, could not improve upon Gooch's efforts.

As ever, Gooch greeted his milestones lugubriously, keeping his feelings tightly private. He is a misunderstood man, not a natural communicator and yet, among people he knows and trusts, a very witty man too. He is a model professional, giving his all to whatever cause is occupying him, and if some of his most notable innings have been against the old enemy Australia (including his highest Test score of 196, at The Oval in 1985) his remarkable, consistent record against the West Indies during their decade of ascendancy, is the most valuable testimony to his ability.

In the latter half of the 1980s, England came to rely ever more heavily upon him as their most dependable blunter of opposition attacks, a man admired by colleagues and hugely respected by bowlers around the world. In an age of bowling domination in Test cricket, the fact that he steadily improved his batting average was a measure of his maturity.

David Gower

Record

David Ivon Gower was born at Tunbridge Wells, Kent, on 1 April 1957. A left-handed, middle-order batsman, he made his debut for Leicestershire at the age of 18 and was playing for England by the time he was 21. The Australian tour of 1978–9 was his first of nine in succession, two as England captain, and in the home series against West Indies in 1988, he played his 100th Test Match, during which his batting average has never fallen below 40. In addition, he has played more than 100 one-day internationals. His highest score is 215, made against Australia at Edgbaston in 1985. He is now in his second spell as captain of Leicestershire.

‘ If David Gower was an Australian, he'd be in my team every time ’

Allan Border, 1985

Technique

Of all the quality players to have represented England in the last 20 years, no one has made batting look so ridiculously easy as David Gower. When in his best touch, he appears to caress the ball to the boundary rather than striking it, and he has the rare ability to make a good-length ball resemble a half-volley. His critics, however, will complain that there are times when he makes a wide half-volley resemble an unplayable delivery. Such is the enigma of the man.

His greatest asset is timing, an instinct or gift rather than something which can easily be acquired. Practice will obviously sharpen the timing of the most modest player, although Gower has tended to treat nets as a necessary chore rather than a place to work on improvements. He will practise because he feels he should, rather than because he wants to, or because he believes it will benefit him. This adds to the impression that he is a lazy cricketer, although in truth he is nowhere near as casually indifferent to his game as he sometimes seems.

Gower can play with equal facility off front or back foot. His most identifiable strokes are the cover drive, which he plays with a grace not seen from any England batsman since the days of Graveney and Cowdrey, and the drive through mid-wicket, all down to his timing.

The leg-glance can be played according to the field-setting. Here, Gower is working the ball just behind square with the full face of the bat. Played later, and more delicately, it will send the ball finer

HIGHLIGHTS 🏆

Captaincy has weighed down many a cricketer. The history of the game is crammed full of examples of players who have suffered from the extra responsibility, losing their individual form and, subsequently, their confidence. For a time, it seemed that Gower would be joining the list, for at the start of the 1985 home series with Australia he was desperately short of runs; many were only too willing to blame the fact that he was England captain. Come the end of the summer, he had dispelled all such notions in brilliant style with a remarkable series aggregate of 732 runs and an average of 81.33.

With Mike Gatting, Graham Gooch and Tim Robinson also averaging more than 50 in the six-Test series, it was something of a golden summer for England batsmanship. In the years to come, however, it will be Gower who is best remembered, for the elegant, assured manner in which he emerged from a personal crisis.

He was at his lowest ebb after two of the limited-overs internationals at the start of the season. Australia had won them both, against expectations, and Gower's scores had been 3 and 0. In the final game, at Lord's, he began like a man dreadfully out of form but showed a tenacity many had imagined to be beyond him in fighting through to a time when his touch returned. He scored 102, England won easily, and his summer changed course from that day on.

England won the first Test, Australia the second. Gower scored 166 in the next game, but two draws brought the series to a palpitating climax. No one was quite prepared for what followed – two massive England victories, each by an innings, with the captain dominating proceedings. He scored 215 on the Edgbaston ground where, seven years earlier, he had pulled his first ball in Test cricket for four. Then, at The Oval on a blazingly hot late August day, he scored 157 of a second-wicket stand of 351 with Gooch. English cricket, and Gower in particular, ended the season on an unaccustomed high. Everyone who enjoys fluent stroke-play would like to remember Gower as he was then.

GORDON GREENIDGE

RECORD 📖

Cuthbert Gordon Greenidge was born in St Peter, on the Caribbean island of Barbados, on 1 May 1951. A right-handed, opening batsman, he came to England with his family at the age of 12 and was educated in Reading, Berkshire. He joined Hampshire in 1970 and played for them until 1987, scoring consistently and setting many records in limited-overs cricket. On his debut for the West Indies, in Bangalore at the age of 23, he scored 93 and 107 against India. He has been their first-choice opener ever since and, fitness permitting, could soon join the elite few to have played 100 Test Matches. His highest Test score remains the 223 he made against England at Manchester in 1984. He was made an MBE in 1985.

> ❛ Greenidge batted with the air of a man in control of every situation ❜
>
> *Wisden*, 1985

TECHNIQUE 🏏

If the argument that English county cricket acts as a breeding ground for other countries' Test stars is valid, then Gordon Greenidge is the persuasive evidence. He joined Hampshire as a teenager, long before he was even known in the Caribbean, and his formidable batting talents were honed in the county's exciting side of the early 70s, when Greenidge formed an inspiring opening partnership with the brilliant South African, Barry Richards.

Greenidge learned a lot from Richards. Early on, he was an impatient aggressor, who wanted to flog bowling to all parts. He learned the merits of building an innings from the elegant springbok who, at his peak, was a hungry collector of major scores. To his impressive array of attacking strokes, Greenidge added a technically immaculate defence which has served him well on the contrasting Test pitches around the world for the past 15 years.

His footwork is quick and positive, whether going smartly back to unwind a savage cut or hook against the quick bowler, or dancing down the pitch to loft the spinner straight back over his head. His range of shots is such that, when he is in the mood, he can render any bowling

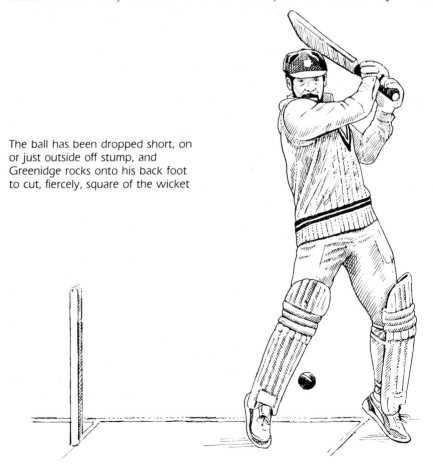

The ball has been dropped short, on or just outside off stump, and Greenidge rocks onto his back foot to cut, fiercely, square of the wicket

utterly inadequate. In recent years, fielding sides have also grown to dread the moment that Greenidge adopts his familiar limp . . . it is normally the prelude to a century!

HIGHLIGHTS 🏆

Although he has scored heavily off all the major Test-playing countries, Greenidge seems to take special delight in tormenting England's bowling. This is a huge irony, considering he could easily have become an England player. Early in his career with Hampshire, the then England captain Ray Illingworth made a rapid assessment of his potential and recommended that the English authorities approach him; as he had been in the country from an early age, he could quickly have qualified. Greenidge, however, preferred to remain loyal to his native islands, and England have frequently had cause to regret missing out.

Perhaps his greatest achievement came in the Manchester Test of 1976, when the West Indies chose to bat, found the pitch more awkward than they expected, and quickly subsided to 26 for four, three wickets falling to Mike Selvey on his England debut. Greenidge survived and took command, his 134 out of 211 forming 63.5 per cent of the West Indies' total, the second highest proportion in Test history. After England had been skittled out for 71, Greenidge then scored 101 in the second innings, only the second man to score a century in each innings of a Test between these countries. The West Indies won the game by 425 runs and Greenidge could hardly have done more towards it.

Eight years later, during the 1984 series which England were ultimately to lose by a humiliating 5–0, David Gower's side maintained a thread of control for the first four days of the Second Test at Lord's. Gower even dared to declare on the final morning, setting the visitors an intimidating 342 in five and a half hours. The hopes of the nation were high, but Greenidge shot them down in remorseless style, hitting no fewer than 29 fours in a ruthless exhibition of stroke-play. He finished up with 214 not out and the West Indies won by nine wickets with more than half an hour to spare. Many consider this the finest innings of Greenidge's life – but the candidates for that award are many and varied.

Desmond Haynes

Record 📖

Desmond Leo Haynes was born in the village of St James, Barbados on 15 February 1956. A right-handed, opening batsman, he first appeared in the all-conquering Barbados island side at the age of 20 and, a year later, he was opening the West Indies innings with Gordon Greenidge, another Barbadian, for the first time. Haynes made half-centuries in each of his first three Test innings and, although his Test career was interrupted by a year spent in World Series Cricket, his partnership with Greenidge has become the most enduring and consistent in world cricket. Haynes, who has never played English county cricket, had his finest moment at Lord's in 1980, when scoring 184 against England and sharing a second-wicket stand of 223 with Viv Richards. He has now scored more than 4,500 runs in Test cricket.

‘ Beneath the carefree exterior lies a very serious and dedicated player ’

Technique 🏏

All those who believe that cricketers from the Caribbean fall into a pattern might be surprised by Desmond Haynes. To look at, he is the typical West Indian batsman – the lithe, laughing cavalier. But beneath the carefree exterior lies a very serious and dedicated player who has learned that to prosper in the jungle of Test cricket these days, you first need to survive. His defence, which might once have seemed secondary to his youthful aggression, is now his main ally in his primary job of seeing off the new-ball onslaught of opposing Test Match attacks.

He is predominantly a back-foot player, happiest on hard, fast pitches where the ball comes truly on to the bat. His success in England, however, confirms that he has mastered the slower, seaming pitches and the moving ball encountered in this country, despite being one of few recent West Indian stars who have preferred not to commit themselves to the demanding county circuit.

None of this should suggest that Haynes has become strokeless. He is a fine, classical driver, hitting through the ball with head studiously low, and when the ball is short he can cut and pull to savage effect. His passport to prolonged success, however, has been the acquisition of a patient, implacable temperament which can withstand many hours of concentration in the search for a match-winning score.

HIGHLIGHTS 🏆

The popular image of Barbados was embodied in Des Haynes when he literally came off the beach to play his first international cricket in the strife-torn winter of 1977–8. Cricket had been split by the Kerry Packer crisis and Haynes, just 22 years old, was one of the most prized young talents. He signed for Packer – but not before he had left an indelible impression of great things to come by scoring 61, 66 and 55 in his first three Test innings against Australia.

Two years later, back in the official West Indian side after the calling of a truce in the damaging battle between Packer and the establishment, Haynes toured Australia and New Zealand. It was in the latter country that he was to make his name in what, for a West Indian cricketer of recent times, was a most unusual way. Probably the greatest heroics of his life were performed in a losing cause, on the bleak ground at Carisbrook, Dunedin.

This was a match most West Indians have been happy to forget – a dramatic one-wicket defeat by the lowly rated New Zealanders, in which various of Clive Lloyd's team disgraced themselves by truculent behaviour. Haynes stayed aloof from the petulance and played two of the most correct and disciplined innings of his career in becoming the first man in history to bat throughout both innings of a Test Match.

Adjusting his technique to counter the suspect pitch and movement off the seam, Haynes took guard outside his crease and consistently played forward. He made 55 out of 140 before being last man out in the first innings; then, after New Zealand had taken a lead of 109, he kept his team in contention by scoring 105 in seven and a quarter hours. New Zealand set a mere 104 to win, scrambled home with their last pair together, thanks to a leg bye. But for Haynes, the reformed beach boy turned heroic blocker, the West Indies would have been more thoroughly humiliated.

GRAEME HICK

RECORD 📖

Graeme Ashley Hick was born in Salisbury, Rhodesia (now Harare, Zimbabwe) on 23 May 1966. A right-handed batsman, usually at number three, he was included in Zimbabwe's party for the 1983 World Cup at the age of 17, making him the youngest ever participant. After a year in the Midland leagues he made his debut for Worcestershire in 1984 and has since carried all before him. In 1986 he became the youngest player to score 2,000 runs in an English first-class season; in 1988 he was the youngest to score 1,000 before the end of May, helped by a phenomenal innings of 405 against Somerset at Taunton. He ended the 1988 season with 2,713 first-class runs, averaging 77.51, having inspired Worcestershire to the 'double' of Championship and Sunday League. He will be qualified to play Test cricket for England in 1991.

❛ I count myself fortunate to have played with two truly great batsmen, Viv Richards and Graeme Hick ❜

Ian Botham, 1988

TECHNIQUE 🏏

There is an old saying in cricket about doing the simple things well. Graeme Hick does the simple things so unusually well that he has been hailed as one of the finest players the world has seen, even before he has had the opportunity to play Test cricket. Although his talent and his figures are extraordinary, his method is not. It is a classical, textbook technique which relies on the fundamentals of bringing the bat down straight, keeping the head still and the weight balanced. It sounds very easy and, indeed, Hick makes it look quite ridiculously easy.

Hick is very far from being a flashy stroke-maker. His reputation and his record is founded on a rock-solid defence, honed by many hours of diligent practice. He will assault selectively, but when he does release his armoury of shots, the results are worth travelling a long way and paying a substantial admission charge to see.

He intimidates the opposition even before taking guard, striding out from the pavilion so rapidly that he is usually at the crease before the dismissed batsman has left the ground. Urgency and conviction are mirrored in everything he does. His strokes are crafted with care; casualness has no place in his portfolio. He plays every stroke bar the hook, preferring to pull low in front of square but perhaps the most striking blows are his straight and on-drives and his delicate late cut.

The late cut is a neglected stroke these days but, properly played, it is a delight. No-one does it better than Hick, his sensitive timing almost caressing the ball on its way between slip and gully

HIGHLIGHTS ♆

Not too many batsmen can claim to have made their first century at the age of six. This, however, is just one of many curiously impressive statistics lining the cricketing life of the modest Hick. He was playing for Banket Primary School against Mangula Juniors and his 105 not out included no fewer than 96 in boundaries. Time has told that this was no fluke, simply a hint of what was to come.

When he played in the Zimbabwe side which toured England in 1985, his first two innings produced 230 against Oxford University and 192 against Glamorgan. The following winter he went home to his family and intended only to coach in the local schools. But an Irish national team, on tour in Zimbabwe, mildly complained about the poor standard of opposition they were meeting. Zimbabwe's answer was to recruit Hick, who scored 155 not out in the next one-day game, followed by 309, a Zimbabwean record, in the three-day international. There were no further mutterings from the Irish.

It is hardly surprising that Worcestershire team-mates soon came to refer to Hick as 'Roy of the Rovers'. His exploits really did rival those of the famous, comic-book football star. Some of them were frankly incredible, never more so than in the early weeks of the 1988 season. Worcestershire's first match was at Old Trafford against Lancashire, quietly fancied for the Championship and quietly fancying that they had the measure of this young upstart. They believed he was suspect against spin. Hick proved them hideously wrong. On a pitch prepared for the slow bowlers, turning extravagantly from the opening morning, he scored a masterly 212. Then, to add insult to injury, he helped bowl Lancashire to defeat with his own off-breaks.

Two weeks later came the most phenomenal innings of the year, if not the decade. Hick's unbeaten 405 fell just 19 runs short of the highest score ever recorded in an English first-class match – 93 years earlier and ironically also at Taunton. Typically, the fact that declaration had deprived him of the record did not bother Hick one bit. He had the team in mind, which is what makes him such an agreeably brilliant batsman.

ALVIN KALLICHARRAN

RECORD 📖

Alvin Isaac Kallicharran was born in Paidama, British Guiana on 21 March 1949. A left-handed batsman, only 5 feet 4 inches tall but wristy and quick-footed, he played 66 times for the West Indies between 1971 and 1981, captaining his country nine times. His Test career ended with a life ban for his part in the 'rebel' West Indies tours to South Africa, but he continued to play in county cricket for Warwickshire, where he has for some years lived with his wife and son, Rohan. His Test career began sensationally, with scores of 100 not out and 101 in his first two innings, against the 1971 New Zealanders, and in all he scored 12 Test centuries and more than 4,000 Test runs before taking a conscious decision to split his cricket between England and South Africa, where he has played with great success for Transvaal and Orange Free State.

'He gets in line and plays straight, which is the starting point to success'

TECHNIQUE 🏏

Now and again in the course of cricket history has arrived a batsman to prove that lack of height is no bar to greatness. Rohan Kanhai was one such miniature giant. Kallicharran, who ploughed the same furrow between Guyana, Warwickshire and the West Indies, is quite definitely another. He looks frail, boyish and vulnerable when he walks into bat but the impression is swiftly banished by first sight of his skills.

Like all of the best batsmen, a correct technique is his most valuable virtue. He gets in line and plays straight, which is the starting point to success. To these fundamentals, Kallicharran could add a natural, instinctive flair for attack, often executed with a power quite breathtakingly savage from one so small. In the World Cup of 1975 he gave a classical case in point, climaxing the West Indies' group stage win over market rivals Australia with a staggering assault on Dennis Lillee which brought him 35 off ten deliveries, including a six and seven fours. He was named Man of the Match there, and again in the semi-final, where once more he gave a dazzling exhibition of the hooks and pulls he has always played to such perfection.

Although predominantly a back-foot player against fast bowling, Kallicharran is quick and nimble in using his feet against the spinners and has no hesitation in hitting them back over their head. His mastery

A master of the hook and pull, note that Kallicharran swivels on his back foot, keeps his eyes on the ball and turns the wrists to keep the ball down

of slow-bowling was exemplified in the winter of 1978–9 when, as captain of the West Indies, he averaged almost 60 in a losing series in India.

HIGHLIGHTS ♟

He came from humble roots in the backwoods of Guyana and, like many a modern-day West Indian star, he learned his cricket the homespun way, batting with a stick against an improvised ball on any patch of waste ground. He needed to be determined; he also needed the support of his family. He was one of 11 children and his father, who farmed in rice and coconut, captained the local Port Mourant club. It was, however, an uncle, a shopkeeper in the town, who gave him the dollar a week he needed to meet the cricket club subscriptions and further his passion. It is a romantic background to a career story which has subsequently suffered all manner of turbulence.

The controversies are extreme. In one, he was rewarded for loyalty by being given the West Indies captaincy. In another, he was punished for defection by a life ban. The first episode came in 1977 when Kallicharran, naive and uninformed as were so many others, signed up for Kerry Packer's World Series Cricket circuit without knowing the possible consequences. Once he realised what it might entail, and what damage it could do to his existing contracts and his attempts to become a British citizen, he dramatically withdrew. West Indies, having lost virtually a complete team to the breakaway group, made 'Kalli' captain. Four years later, he ignored pleas from the Caribbean and took up a contract with Transvaal in South Africa's Currie Cup, knowing it would bring about the end of his Test career. His later involvement with the rebel tours of South Africa made doubly sure his West Indies days were over.

Probably the most explosive incident to involve this cheerful character, however, was in Trinidad during the 1973–4 Test Match against England. Kallicharran was past 100 and going well when the last ball of the first day was played to square-leg. There was no chance of a run, so Kallicharran, at the non-striker's end, began walking towards the pavilion, whereupon Tony Greig threw down the stumps and appealed. The hapless umpire, Douglas Sang Hue, correctly adjudged the batsman out but after some ugly crowd scenes, and the threat of worse to come, diplomacy dictated that the decision should be reversed. Kallicharran went out to resume his innings next day.

ALLAN LAMB

RECORD 📖

Allan Joseph Lamb was born in Langebaanweg, Cape Province, South Africa on 20 June 1954. A stocky, powerful, middle-order, right-hand batsman and fine outfielder, he qualified for England in 1982, through having British parents, and was instantly chosen for the national side, making 107 against India in only his third Test match. He had been a regular in the Western Province Currie Cup side in his native South Africa since 1972 and joined Northamptonshire in 1978. His record in limited-overs internationals is better than his Test figures, although when confronted by the ultimate examination against the West Indian pace bowlers he has been superb, scoring three centuries in the 5–0 defeat of 1984 and another in 1988.

‘ Lamb stout-heartedly proceeded to douse West Indies' fire ’

Wisden, 1985

TECHNIQUE

The batting philosophy of Allan Lamb has always been refreshingly straightforward. He believes you should look to dominate and, if possible, to score from every ball faced. This is a route fraught with danger but it guarantees entertainment. Lamb has always been an exciting, invigorating batsman to watch because he plays each innings as he likes to live his life, the bold adventurer scoffing at the negative and the lethargic.

For this reason it is better to concentrate on his attacking repertoire rather than his defence which, while good enough to sustain him as a top-class player, is flawed in strict textbook terms. He learned his cricket on the hard, fast wickets of South Africa and, like most who emerge from such schooling, he became an instinctive stroke-maker who trusted his eye and his judgement. He needed time, though not much, to adapt to the less trustworthy pitches of England and he has always been most comfortable when batting in circumstances which allow him to play his natural, attacking game.

He has only a short backlift and he prefers to play off the back foot, despite professing a flourishing on-drive which has earned him many boundaries. He is at his best, perhaps, against bowling which is short of a length, working the straight ones into gaps for scurried singles and launching fierce cuts, drives and pulls against anything a little wider. This facility gives the key to his remarkable success against the West Indian fast bowlers.

HIGHLIGHTS 🏆

Allan Lamb has a long-standing love affair with Lord's, the headquarters of English cricket in the leafy London district of St John's Wood. He admits to finding the setting inspiring, and his record on the ground proves it. In 1980, his first major match in English cricket was the Benson and Hedges Cup Final, in which he played for Northampton-shire against Essex. Lamb's 72 was the decisive contribution to a surprise victory. 'I love the big occasion,' he said afterwards and, in years to come, he was to love each return to Lord's. Of his eight Test Match centuries by the end of 1988, three of them had been made at HQ.

The first two were in 1984. At the end of that summer he scored 107 in England's first home Test against Sri Lanka, but the innings which gave him more pleasure came in late June against the West Indies. It was a century which briefly hinted at a breakthrough in England's fight to shake off the utter dominance exerted by Clive Lloyd's great side. England had taken a first-innings lead of 41 thanks to the superb bowling of Ian Botham. Then Lamb set to work, correcting a potential disaster at 33 for three and defying Joel Garner and Malcolm Marshall for six hours. When he was out for 110 England actually declared, whereupon Gordon Greenidge mocked the stiff target of 342.

If this was heartbreak for Lamb, there was more agony to follow at the hands of the West Indies. Twice more, during that 1984 series, he scored battling hundreds in a lost cause. Four years later he was at it again. Lamb had been out of the England side for some while, his form having lapsed, but England wisely backed his pugnacity against the West Indies and his passion for Lord's. He did not let them down. As England chased an apparently impossible 442 to win a rollercoaster match, Lamb kept the dream alive. No one else in the team managed more than 30 but Lamb battled on to 113 before tragically being run out. Overall, he may not quite have fulfilled his potential at Test Level – but try telling that to the West Indies, or even to the Long Room regulars at Lord's.

CLIVE LLOYD

RECORD

Clive Hubert Lloyd was born in Georgetown, Guyana on 31 August 1944. A left-handed, middle-order batsman and, in his early years, medium-pace bowler, he played for his native Guyana for 21 years up to 1983 but has now made his permanent home in England. A Lancashire player from 1968 until 1986, and captain of the county for four years, he enjoyed a glittering career as batsman and captain of the West Indies, supervising their transformation from an erratic, emotional side to the team which terrorised all-comers during the late 1970s and the 1980s. Lloyd played 110 Tests, scoring 7,515 runs, second only to Gary Sobers among West Indians. He captained his country 74 times, of which 36 Tests were won – both figures a record. He is now retired from playing and acts as manager of the West Indian side.

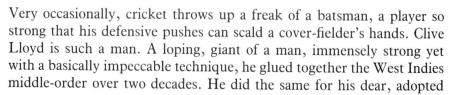

'A natural leader, a gifted statesman, he was also an extremely fine batsman'

TECHNIQUE

Very occasionally, cricket throws up a freak of a batsman, a player so strong that his defensive pushes can scald a cover-fielder's hands. Clive Lloyd is such a man. A loping, giant of a man, immensely strong yet with a basically impeccable technique, he glued together the West Indies middle-order over two decades. He did the same for his dear, adopted

Lancashire, where Mancunians now regard him as 'one of us'. He was a player who commanded the respect of players and the adoration of spectators around the world. A natural leader, a gifted statesman, he was also an extremely fine batsman in his own right.

If the power came from his 14-stone frame as well as his timing, then his great height – 6 feet 5 inches – also played a large part in his cricketing success. He was a schoolboy athletic champion back in Guyana and he found that his unusually long arms and legs had their uses on the cricket field, too. He became a quite outstanding cover fielder until a deteriorating knee injury sent him into the slips for the rest of his career and, with the bat, his method was based around his phenomenal reach. Lloyd could turn an apparently good-length ball into a friendly half-volley, and did so frequently. When in the mood, his driving, both off front and back foot, was a stunning sight, and although he batted in glasses for most of his career, he was also a brilliant hooker. Once, at The Oval in a county match for Lancashire, he hooked a ball from Robin Jackman out of the ground and over the neighbouring road into a garden – a distance reckoned to be about 150 yards. He will long be remembered for his flamboyance but, when events dictated, he could also defend masterfully.

HIGHLIGHTS 🏆

Clive Lloyd was an inspiration behind Lancashire's domination of limited-overs cricket two decades ago. Between 1969 and 1972 they won the Sunday League twice and the Gillette Cup (as it was then called) three times in succession. So it was only natural that when one-day cricket spread its wings on the international circuit, Lloyd should be a major force. In 1975, the World Cup was staged for the first time. It was a tentative experiment, frowned upon by many traditionalists. Lloyd converted them all on the longest day of the summer and one of the longest days of cricket ever played.

The final matched Australia and the West Indies, just as the pre-tournament seedings had indicated. The West Indies, whose reputation then was nowhere near as high and established as it is now, began badly, losing Fredericks, Greenidge and Kallicharran for only 50 to the Australian pace attack, which included both Lillee and Thomson. Lloyd strode in, and the game altered course with dramatic certainty.

It needs a very special cricketer to take a game by the scruff of the neck, let alone a game of such historical moment and tension. Lloyd, in that deceptively casual style, asserted himself as if he was playing on a village green. Lillee, pumped up with aggression, dropped short. Lloyd hooked him square for six. The die was cast. Soon, the Australians had lost control. In less than two hours, Lloyd scored 102, spurring his team to an imposing score of 291 for eight in their 60 overs. Then, despite a brave fightback by Australia, he coolly led the West Indies to the victory which set them on the path to their dominance of world cricket. Lloyd was made Man of the Match, just before 9pm on a wonderfully sunny evening. It was a day nobody present in the capacity crowd will ever forget, and you may be sure Lloyd will count it among his most treasured memories and most influential days.

JAVED MIANDAD

RECORD

Javed Miandad Khan was born in Karachi, Pakistan on June 12th, 1957. A right-handed middle-order batsman and occasional leg-spinner, he has two brothers who both played provincial cricket in Pakistan. He made his first-class debut, for Karachi, at the age of 16 and played his first Test Match when only 19, scoring 163 against New Zealand. By the age of 22 he had already made six Test hundreds and was being acclaimed as a genius. He played county cricket for Sussex for four years and then spent seven seasons with Glamorgan, including one year as their captain. He has also had three separate spells as captain of Pakistan. He once made 311 for Karachi Whites against the National Bank and has amassed several double-centuries, including 280 not out against India and 260 against England. He is the highest run-scorer in Pakistan's Test history and averages more than 50 in Test cricket.

❝ Javed is an excellent player of spin bowling, even on bad pitches. He likes taking risks ❞

Imran Khan

TECHNIQUE

In one of less talent, Javed Miandad's instincts would have been his undoing. At the crease he is ambitious and impatient, like a chained dog straining for release. His answer is often improvisation and yet, such is his brilliance, he makes poetic runs out of situations where others would end up in undignified disaster.

Miandad is confident. He is perhaps even arrogant, certainly a shade cocky. It does not make him the most universally popular opponent but it does give him a priceless head start – he believes he is good enough to dominate any attack and, now and again, he is able to transmit his self-assurance to the bowlers, disarming and demoralising them.

His great gifts are his eyes and his feet, all four of which are nimble and accurate. Few, if any of the world's top batsmen pick length better and then react more swiftly. Miandad can turn a good length ball into a half-volley with one of his typical darts down the pitch. He drives through extra-cover with flourish, the widening grin on his face both an expression of his own joy and an assured irritant to the suffering bowler.

A safe, adroit and economical player of the quickest bowling, Miandad can be at his most spectacular against spin. John Emburey, England's foremost slow bowler of the past decade, believes he is the most difficult

Miandad has never felt bound by the text book. He is the game's premier inventor, mischief in every stroke. Here, typically, he demonstrates a risky but profitable shot, stepping away to cut the spinner behind square, the back foot anchored

man in the world to contain. He refuses to be tied to his crease but, when he chooses to stay, he will sweep, cut and glance into space with incredible precision. A true artist.

HIGHLIGHTS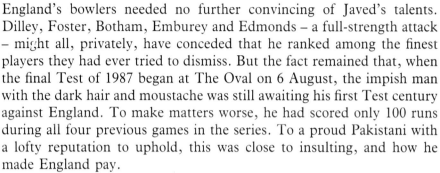

England's bowlers needed no further convincing of Javed's talents. Dilley, Foster, Botham, Emburey and Edmonds – a full-strength attack – might all, privately, have conceded that he ranked among the finest players they had ever tried to dismiss. But the fact remained that, when the final Test of 1987 began at The Oval on 6 August, the impish man with the dark hair and moustache was still awaiting his first Test century against England. To make matters worse, he had scored only 100 runs during all four previous games in the series. To a proud Pakistani with a lofty reputation to uphold, this was close to insulting, and how he made England pay.

The scenario was this: after two rain-affected draws, Pakistan had won the Third Test at Headingley by an innings. With the fourth match also drawn, England were threatened with their first ever home series defeat by Pakistan. Miandad, with sterling assistance from his inspirational captain, Imran Khan, guaranteed that there could be no way out for Mike Gatting's team.

Coming in on the first morning at a precarious 45 for two, Miandad batted ten hours and 17 minutes to make 260. It was not his highest score in Test cricket but it was perhaps his most dominant innings. Quite frankly, England's five distinguished bowlers despaired of ever finding a way to get him out and, when he did go, tapping a return catch to the persevering Dilley, it was more through personal fatigue than the skills of the bowler.

This was Miandad's fourth double-century in Test cricket, a feat which puts him in the company of an elite half-dozen. In the process, he also passed 6,000 runs for Pakistan and rebuked anyone who had begun to doubt his extraordinary talent. Emburey, who has gone on record with his high opinions of Miandad's batting, finished with nought for 143, Botham with three for 217. It was a bloodless coup.

Mudassar Nazar

Record

Mudassar Nazar was born in Lahore, Pakistan on 6 April 1956. A right-handed, opening batsman, small but wiry, he made his first-class debut in his native land in 1971–2 and has since played for a number of Pakistan's provincial sides. In addition, although he has never played county cricket, which might well have suited his talents, he has been a regular and very successful professional in the Northern leagues. He made his first appearance for Pakistan against Australia at Adelaide Oval on Christmas Eve, 1976, but after one undistinguished Test he was left out for a full year, returning against England in Lahore, where he scored 114. He has been an established member of the side ever since and has now scored more than 4,000 runs with an average in excess of 40.

‘ He has achieved a lot in Tests through sheer hard work. He is a very intelligent player ’

Imran Khan

Technique

Although he has occasionally batted lower in the order, Mudassar is best suited by going in first. As any opener will confirm, however, it is easier to prosper in the position with an established partner, so that teamwork and understanding can be called into play. Mudassar has been unfortunate in this respect. Starting with Majid Khan in 1976, he has survived a large number of partners and the fact that he is still very much part of the side today is a tribute to his tenacity and skill.

His most profitable period was probably in the early eighties, when Mohsin Khan was his regular ally against the new ball. Mohsin's upright grace and elegance was an effective contrast to the busy, accumulative style favoured by Mudassar. He has never been the most attractive of players to watch but his urgency and purpose are themselves endearing and, despite his unfortunate reputation as something of a slowcoach, he is well equipped to score quickly when the situation demands.

The most obvious point about Mudassar is that he is a team man, a virtue, which can never be overstated. He adapts his own game to suit the needs of the side so that, in one-day cricket, he scores much more quickly and is a very fine judge of quick singles. He has played more than 100 one-day internationals for his country with consistent success both as batsman and bowler.

HIGHLIGHTS 🏆

Late in the October of 1952, the only Test Match ever played in the Indian city of Lucknow was won by Pakistan by an innings. Apart from being played on a matting pitch, the game was notable for one further reason. Nazar Mohammed, opening the batting in only his second Test Match, carried his bat through the Pakistan innings to make 124 not out, thus becoming the first player in history to be on the field for an entire Test Match. His century was a painstaking affair – he batted for almost nine hours – and it was to have a remarkable sequel 25 years later.

Nazar Mohammed was forced to retire from the game in 1953 after suffering a severe arm injury, but he never lost his interest. He became a national coach and, in the fulness of time, one of his star pupils was his own son, Mudassar. The coaching left its mark. In December 1977 Mudassar, also playing only his second Test for Pakistan, scored his maiden century and took so long over it that he entered the record books.

Mudassar batted a total of nine hours, 17 minutes for his century, the slowest ever recorded in Test history. He did not quite emulate his father by being on the field throughout the game but it remains one of the great coincidences of cricket. The sufferers on this occasion were

England, who used six bowlers, including Geoff Boycott, to try and dislodge Mudassar, before he was finally caught and bowled by Geoff Miller for 114. The game, needless to add, was drawn but it still has a special place in cricketing folklore, not to mention in the scrapbooks of the Nazar family. Unlike his father, Mudassar has thankfully avoided serious injuries and is still playing well at the highest level today. Whenever his name is mentioned, however, cricketers recall Lahore, 1978, and the great act of stonewalling.

GRAEME POLLOCK

RECORD 📖

Robert Graeme Pollock was born in Port Elizabeth, South Africa on 27 February 1944. A left-handed middle-order batsman, his first-class career spanned 27 years until his retirement in 1987, at the age of 43. He made his debut for Orange Free State in 1961 and scored his maiden century before his 17th birthday. In all, he totalled more than 20,000 runs at a career average of 54.67. The tragedy of Pollock is that he was restricted, by the isolation of South Africa, to only 23 Test Matches, in which he scored seven centuries and averaged more than 60. His final series was in 1969–70 against Australia. The brilliant, soon redundant South African team won 4–0 and, in the Second Test at Durban, Pollock scored 274, the highest Test innings by a South African.

‘ The abiding memory is likely to be of a crashing straight drive ’

TECHNIQUE 🏏

The last time Graeme Pollock played competitively in England was in 1970. He took part in the five-match series between England and the Rest of the World, designed to substitute for the abandoned visit by South Africa. He must have known in his heart he might never play Test cricket again, but he left England with something to remember him by, scoring a century in the fifth match of the series at The Oval.

Time, however, has cruelly clouded that memory. The youngsters of today never did get to see Pollock, which is their collective loss. He was a genius, a rare, visionary batsman whose strokes were like cut glass in a junk shop. Whatever the company, whatever the strength of opposition, Pollock stood out.

It is invidious to compare him with players of today or yesteryear. Suffice it to say that his boyhood idol was the Australian left-hander, Neil Harvey, while of the current crop of world-class batsman, the Zimbabwean-born Graeme Hick is thought by many to resemble Pollock very closely, except that Hick is right-handed.

Power and elegance are words which describe Pollocks' batting. For those who did scc him play, the abiding memory is likely to be of a crashing straight drive, probably from a good length and well-directed ball. Pollock was no respecter of bowlers' accuracy. He did not need to be, such was his innate judgement and instinct for a stroke.

HIGHLIGHTS 🏆

Trent Bridge, Nottingham, August 1965. South Africa scored the victory which was to bring them their first win in a series in England for 30 years. Their players celebrated in style long after the crowds had left the ground, their drinks toasting two particular heroes . . . the brothers Pollock. Peter Pollock, a strapping fast bowler, had taken ten wickets for 87 in the match. Graeme, three years younger at just 21, had totalled 184 runs in a game where neither side mustered a score above 300. His first-innings efforts brought him 125 and there are those who will still tell you today that they have never seen better batting.

He went in to bat on the opening morning. South Africa were 16 for two, both the wickets having fallen to the canny seam bowler Tom Cartwright, operating in conditions tailor-made for him. Soon, the score was 43 for four and then 80 for five, at which point Pollock was joined by his captain, Peter van der Merwe. Together, they added 98 for the sixth wicket, although in truth van der Merwe's was a strictly passive role. Pollock, having granted lip service to the custom of playing yourself in, astonished the England bowlers and enchanted the crowd with a blistering array of shots. After lunch, he scored 91 out of 102 in just 70 minutes.

Pollock offered not a single semblance of a chance and, more impressive still, he punished the good balls every bit as ferociously as the bad ones. He struck 21 fours, mostly with bludgeoning drives, straight or through cover. He was acclaimed, that very day, as one of the greats, and if his international progress had not been so abruptly cut short, it is perfectly possible that his record would now be comparable with that of Bradman, Sobers and Richards.

VIV RICHARDS

RECORD 📖

Isaac Vivian Alexander Richards was born in the Antiguan capital of St John's on 7 March 1952. A right-handed batsman and occasional slow or slow-medium bowler, he first played for his native Leeward Islands, in the Caribbean's Shell Shield, at the age of 19. He joined Somerset in 1974 and spent 13 seasons at Taunton – his benefit, in 1982, raised £56,440. He graduated to the West Indies side in the winter of 1974–5 and has been an automatic selection ever since. In 1976, he scored 1,710 runs in 11 Test Matches during the calendar year. He succeeded Clive Lloyd as captain of the West Indies in the spring of 1985.

❝ It would be the nearest you could get to a cricketers' paradise to see Richards and Bradman together at the wicket ❞

Tom Graveney

TECHNIQUE 🏏

The way in which Viv Richards saunters to the wicket, his bat swinging alongside him like a toff's umbrella, graphically transmits the power of self-confidence. If his innermost thoughts remain strictly private, the image he sells the viewer and, more importantly, the opposition, is that of a superior being consenting to come along and sort out a little local uprising. There are other players whose authority is obvious from their stroke-play but surely none who can intimidate and dismay before they have so much as taken guard. Richards' unspoken message to the bowlers is that he will score as many runs as he sees fit before giving them a chance. Quite how many runs his manner has been worth to him, over the years, is not quantifiable; sadly for the bowlers, he has a dazzling armoury of shots with which to back it up.

As with all the genuine great players, Richards has an immaculate technique. The resources are there to destroy an attack, and the urge is seldom too far away, but when the need arises, Richards will defend with a ramrod-straight bat and perfectly positioned feet. Then, quite without warning, the tempo of his innings will change, often with a lavish step down the pitch to dispatch a ball of good length past mid-on for four. They say the on-drive is the mark of a good player; no one

It looks easy but timing and balance are essential to the execution of the lofted straight drive. Contact is made 'on the up' rather than half-volley, and note the stillness of the head.

alive executes it quite as well as Richards. Later, if he is in the mood to dominate, his eye for the length of a ball carries him through. He will divert from the textbook to demonstrate his own delightful improvisations. At times, it seems he is an impossible player to contain.

HIGHLIGHTS 🏆

A local Antiguan umpire, applying a little discretionary bias, can probably claim responsibility for launching Viv Richards' long and successful English career with Somerset. Early in 1974 Len Creed, a west country cricket fanatic, took his own touring team to Antigua for a few matches. He took with him a note from former England captain Colin Cowdrey, recommending that he should have a look at a young batsman named Richards. Creed was an unofficial talent scout for Somerset and he was delighted when Richards turned up in the opposition to his own team. He was not so impressed when he appeared to be plainly stumped without scoring . . . but the umpire, who had heard that English eyes were watching his friend Vivian, rejected the appeal. Viv went on to make a decent score and Creed brought him back to Somerset.

Now, Len Creed is a bookmaker and, as everyone is aware, bookies are supposed to be tough, mean and hard-nosed. This one, however, had put his neck on the line in persuading Somerset that this unknown West Indian was a star of the future, and Richards recalls that when he left the Swansea ground after making 81 not out on his county debut, Creed greeted him in tears – tears of joy and relief.

Richards shared a flat in Taunton with Ian Botham. Neither was well-known at the time and it is one of cricket's most compelling tales that these two cavaliers of the crease grew up in the game together, inseparable off the field and irrepressible on it, both watched over by the disciplinarian Somerset captain, Brian Close.

In the subsequent years, Richards has made many memorable hundreds, sometimes turning them into double-hundreds and once, at The Oval against England in 1976, making a marvellous 291. Often, his most striking innings have been the cameos, the furious fifties when no time has been squandered on preliminaries. Now, as captain of the West Indies, his responsibilities are heavier but his skills remain unimpaired. He is a fiercely proud Antiguan, proud of his island, his race and his team – a truly formidable opponent and arguably the best batsman of the 1980s.

DILIP VENGSARKAR

RECORD 📖

Dilip Balwant Vengsarkar was born in Bombay, India on 6 April 1956. A tall, right-handed, middle-order batsman, he is a fine example of a player whose performances have steadily improved throughout his career to a point where he has become the most consistently productive international run-scorer in the world. Early in his cricket career he was considered an opener but later became a specialist number three before, in later years, dropping to four. Until 1986 his Test Match average was some way below 40 but over the next two years he accumulated runs ravenously, averaging more than 100 over the period, including two centuries in three Tests against the West Indies during his brief spell as captain of India, interrupted by injury and then a domestic suspension. He is now leading his country again.

❛ He collects big scores as others collect stamps ❜

TECHNIQUE

One of the hallmarks of greatness in a batsman is the ability to consistently play the ball late. This does not mean jabbing at it at the last possible second; the complete opposite. It means being in position early yet adjusting the timing and placement of the shot once it has finished its lateral movement. Of all the fine players in the world today, few achieve this more effectively, yet more unobtrusively, than Dilip Vengsarkar.

India's captain is a master of the instinct which guides all top batsmen. Yet he is not a memorable big hitter nor is he a batsman whose manner-isms at the crease set him apart from others. He collects big scores as others collect stamps and does so with such quiet command that many people were astonished when confronted with his record over recent years – a record which, since 1986, makes him the most prolific batsman in the world.

His technique is classical. It could have been extracted straight from the coaching manual. He favours neither front nor back foot but is splendidly balanced. His height is an advantage against quick bowling and his judgement of length and movement is superb. It is said that the biggest test of a batsman's technical skills will always arise on English pitches, where the ball deviates so much more than it does overseas. Dilip Vengsarkar has few equals here. He has scored a century on each of his three Test appearances at Lord's and, in 1986, made 61 and 102 not out at Leeds as England were dismissed for 102 and 128 on a deplorable pitch. This was batting of peerless quality.

HIGHLIGHTS 🏆

It takes more than technical excellence to make a batting star in the demanding world of modern Test cricket. It takes a high degree of courage, too, and this is a commodity which Vengsarkar displayed to the full in the very first year of his Test career.

He had enjoyed the best possible schooling, in all senses. His home overlooked a major club cricket ground in Bombay; he went to King George School, which has produced a number of Indian Test players; then, when he left school, he joined the Dadar Union club and found himself playing alongside the great Sunil Gavaskar. He learned well and he learned fast. In January 1976, still only 19, he made his Test debut against New Zealand – as Gavaskar's opening partner. He was out for 7 and 6. It was not the most glorious start and nor was he noticeably more successful in his next three Tests. It was then that India dropped him down to the middle-order, where he has flourished for the rest of his career. The merit of the decision was instantly evident. At Kingston, Jamaica, on a newly relaid pitch of horrifyingly inconsistent bounce,

India's batsmen were tormented by the West Indian attack of Michael Holding, Wayne Daniel and Bernard Julien. Three were injured in the first innings and the captain, Bishan Bedi, deliberately declared as a protest against the short-pitched bowling. The second innings closed at 97 for five, Bedi either declaring again or deciding no one else was fit to bat – it was not clear which. But Vengsarkar had stood erect and brave during both innings. He totalled only 60 in the match but his reputation was made. At a time when India, with no fast bowling ammunition of their own, were thought an easy target by opposing fast bowlers, Vengsarkar refused to be intimidated. It was another ten years before his career reached its peak, but it is a safe bet that he still remembers Jamaica, 1976 with a touch of pride.

JOHN WRIGHT

RECORD 📖

John Geoffrey Wright was born in Darfield, New Zealand on 5 July 1954. A left-handed, opening batsman, tall and solidly built, he graduated from the University of Otago with a degree in Biochemistry and was 21 before he made his first-class debut, for Northern Districts. Derbyshire took him on, in preference to some gifted young South Africans including Allan Lamb, in 1977 and he played happily and successfully there for the next 12 years. He made his New Zealand debut against England in February 1978 and has been their regular, reliable number one ever since. He has now scored more than 3,000 Test Match runs and, early in 1988, he was made New Zealand captain.

❛His application often seems inexhaustible, his determination immense❜

TECHNIQUE

Left-handers are sometimes thought to have an advantage. Being in the minority, they tend to profit more from lapses of direction by bowlers. While the ball angled across the left-hander, from leg to off, causes many a dismissal, it can also be a gift for the adept cover-driver. Similarly deliveries straying fractionally to the leg-side are a source of comfort as the left-handed breed punch through the onside with mechanical regularity. John Wright is no exception to all this. A chart showing the strokes with which he has acquired his runs would show a heavy profit through the square-leg and mid-wicket region. He is also a fine driver of the overpitched ball and in one-day cricket he allows himself the rein to drive in the air over the close field.

In limited-overs cricket, one can see a different player from the John Wright of the Test circuit. He is far more adventurous and aggressive and, as New Zealand's most prolific batsman in one-day internationals, he has played many match-winning innings. His reputation, however, has been built around the ability to sustain technique and concentration for hour after hour in a five-day game. His application often seems inexhaustible, his determination immense. He takes his duties as New Zealand's senior opening batsman extremely seriously, yet remains one of the most sporting and popular cricketers in the world.

HIGHLIGHTS 🏆

For all the sturdy merit of his centuries in Test cricket, John Wright may well regard two narrow failures among his greatest innings. In 1983 he spurred New Zealand to their first Test win in England. In 1988 he very nearly inspired a famous victory over Australia. On both occasions, he was dismissed in the nervous nineties.

The first match was at Headingley, Leeds, on a pitch never ideal for batting. England had been bowled out for 225. New Zealand, sensing a chance to level things up after defeat in the first match of the four-Test series, suffered an early blow when Bruce Edgar, one half of the effective opening team, was hit on the thigh by Botham and forced to retire. Wright dug deep in his resources of patience and courage. He was not helped by two run-outs in which he was arguably culpable but, his tough temperament shining through, he batted almost five hours for 93 to ensure a substantial first-innings lead. New Zealand went on to win by five wickets, a historic achievement following 28 previous attempts at winning in England.

Five years on, New Zealand were under the command of Jeff Crowe in a three-match series in Australia. One down, with only the Christmas Test Match in Melbourne to play, they so nearly saved the series. Crowe lost the toss and New Zealand were put in. Wright, at his most assertive, made sure that this was no disadvantage, making 99 before cruelly falling to a catch behind. New Zealand trailed by 40 on first innings but with all the major batsmen, Wright included, chipping in second time around they were able to set Australia 247 to win. At the end of a nail-biting final day, Australia were 230 for nine and a triumph for which Wright should have taken much credit was denied by the last-wicket pair. Wright, being the man he is, would have swallowed his disappointment, adopted his well-known grin and shared a beer or two with the opposition. A sportsman to the end, he is the type of which cricket could happily do with many more.

CAREER RECORDS

First-class figures are to end of the 1988 English season; Test figures are to 7 February 1989.

A. R. Border

First-class

	Inns.	N.O.	H.S.	Runs	Average	100
	409	62	205	18810	54.20	58

Test cricket

	Inns.	N.O.	H.S.	Runs	Average	100
v. England	57	14	196	2392	55.76	7
v. India	26	1	162	1292	51.68	4
v. New Zealand	22	2	205	1001	50.05	4
v. Pakistan	31	6	153	1532	61.28	6
v. Sri Lanka	2	1	88	135	135.00	–
v. West Indies	41	6	126	1479	42.25	2
TOTAL	179	30	205	7831	52.55	23

I. T. Botham

First-class

	Inns.	N.O.	H.S.	Runs	Average	100
	509	37	228	16422	34.79	33

Test cricket

	Inns.	N.O.	H.S.	Runs	Average	100
v. Australia	55	2	149*	1611	30.39	4
v. India	17	–	208	1201	70.64	5
v. New Zealand	21	2	138	830	43.68	3
v. Pakistan	19	1	108	639	35.50	2
v. Sri Lanka	2	–	13	19	9.50	–
v. West Indies	36	–	81	757	21.02	–
TOTAL	150	5	208	5057	34.87	14

G. Boycott

First-class

	Inns.	N.O.	H.S.	Runs	Average	100
	1014	162	261*	48426	56.83	151

Test cricket

	Inns.	N.O.	H.S.	Runs	Average	100
v. Australia	71	9	191	2945	47.50	7
v. India	22	3	246*	1084	57.05	4
v. New Zealand	25	1	131	916	38.16	2
v. Pakistan	10	3	121*	591	84.42	3
v. South Africa	12	2	117	373	37.30	1
v. West Indies	53	5	128	2205	45.93	5
TOTAL	193	23	246*	8114	47.72	22

M. D. Crowe

First-class

	Inns.	N.O.	H.S.	Runs	Average	100
	274	42	242*	13151	56.68	46

Test cricket

v. Australia	19	2	188	904	53.17	3
v. England	22	2	143	733	36.65	3
v. Pakistan	10	–	84	468	46.80	–
v. Sri Lanka	6	1	45	125	25.00	–
v. West Indies	13	1	188	544	45.33	3
TOTAL	70	6	188	2774	43.34	9

M. W. Gatting

First-class

	Inns	N.O.	H.S.	Runs	Average	100
	526	76	258	21060	46.80	50

Test cricket

v. Australia	33	4	160	1366	47.10	3
v. India	21	6	207	936	62.40	3
v. New Zealand	17	2	121	435	29.00	1
v. Pakistan	27	2	150*	853	34.12	2
v. West Indies	17	–	56	258	15.17	–
TOTAL	115	14	207	3848	38.09	9

S. M. Gavaskar

First-class

	Inns.	N.O.	H.S.	Runs	Average	100
	563	61	340	25834	51.46	81

Test cricket

v. Australia	31	1	172	1550	51.66	8
v. England	67	2	221	2483	38.20	4
v. New Zealand	16	1	119	651	43.40	2
v. Pakistan	41	4	166	2089	56.45	5
v. Sri Lanka	11	2	176	600	66.66	2
v. West Indies	48	6	236*	2749	65.45	13
TOTAL	214	16	236*	10122	51.12	34

Most Tests (125), Test innings (214), Test centuries (34), Test innings over fifty (79)

G. A. Gooch

First-class

	Inns.	N.O.	H.S.	Runs	Average	100
	660	52	275	26745	43.98	66

Test cricket

	Inns.	N.O.	H.S.	Runs	Average	100
v. Australia	40	–	196	1105	27.62	1
v. India	23	2	127	926	44.09	2
v. New Zealand	10	2	183	458	57.25	1
v. Pakistan	8	–	93	299	37.37	–
v. Sri Lanka	4	–	75	164	41.00	–
v. West Indies	38	–	153	1589	41.81	4
TOTAL	123	4	196	4541	38.15	8

D. I. Gower

First-class

	Inns.	N.O.	H.S.	Runs	Average	100
	546	50	215	19890	40.10	40

Test cricket

	Inns.	N.O.	H.S.	Runs	Average	100
v. Australia	56	3	215	2479	46.71	6
v. India	31	4	200*	1100	40.74	1
v. New Zealand	22	1	131	1051	50.04	4
v. Pakistan	22	1	173*	1035	49.28	2
v. Sri Lanka	3	1	89	186	93.00	–
v. West Indies	38	3	154*	1149	32.82	1
TOTAL	172	13	215	7000	44.02	14

C. G. Greenidge

First-class

	Inns.	N.O.	H.S.	Runs	Average	100
	817	69	273*	34440	46.04	83

Test cricket

	Inns.	N.O.	H.S.	Runs	Average	100
v. Australia	43	6	127	1453	39.27	3
v. England	41	2	223	2010	51.53	6
v. India	32	4	194	1435	51.25	4
v. New Zealand	19	3	213	882	55.12	2
v. Pakistan	21	–	100	803	38.23	1
TOTAL	156	15	223	6583	46.68	16

D. L. Haynes

First-class

	Inns.	N.O.	H.S.	Runs	Average	100
	302	33	184	11507	42.77	20

Test cricket

v. Australia	42	4	145	1698	44.68	4
v. England	35	5	184	1481	49.36	3
v. India	25	2	136	710	30.86	1
v. New Zealand	20	3	122	843	49.58	3
v. Pakistan	17	1	88*	328	20.50	–
TOTAL	139	15	184	5060	40.80	11

G. A. Hick

First-class

	Inns.	N.O.	H.S.	Runs	Average	100
	180	16	405*	9681	59.75	34

Test cricket – nil

A. I. Kallicharran

First-class

	Inns.	N.O.	H.S.	Runs	Average	100
	798	83	243*	31819	44.50	85

Test cricket

v. Australia	33	2	127	1325	42.74	4
v. England	24	1	158	891	38.73	2
v. India	25	3	187	1229	55.86	3
v. New Zealand	9	1	101	365	45.62	2
v. Pakistan	18	3	115	589	39.26	1
TOTAL	109	10	187	4399	44.43	12

A. J. Lamb

First-class

	Inns.	N.O.	H.S.	Runs	Average	100
	548	87	294	21756	47.19	55

Test cricket

	Inns.	N.O.	H.S.	Runs	Average	100
v. Australia	27	2	83	814	32.56	–
v. India	16	2	107	513	36.64	1
v. New Zealand	13	2	137*	474	43.09	2
v. Pakistan	11	–	33	126	11.45	–
v. Sri Lanka	3	–	107	178	59.33	1
v. West Indies	28	3	113	864	34.56	4
TOTAL	98	9	137*	2969	33.35	8

C. H. Lloyd

First-class

	Inns.	N.O.	H.S.	Runs	Average	100
	730	96	242*	31232	49.26	79

Test cricket

	Inns.	N.O.	H.S.	Runs	Average	100
v. Australia	48	4	178	2211	50.25	6
v. England	51	4	132	2120	45.10	5
v. India	44	4	242*	2344	58.60	7
v. New Zealand	14	–	44	234	16.71	–
v. Pakistan	18	2	157	606	37.87	1
TOTAL	175	14	242*	7515	46.67	19

Javed Miandad

First-class

	Inns.	N.O.	H.S.	Runs	Average	100
	562	88	311	25400	53.58	72

Test cricket

	Inns.	N.O.	H.S.	Runs	Average	100
v. Australia	35	2	211	1607	48.69	6
v. England	24	4	260	965	48.25	1
v. India	34	6	280*	1949	69.60	4
v. New Zealand	21	5	206	1276	79.75	5
v. Sri Lanka	12	1	203*	545	49.54	1
v. West Indies	20	–	114	691	34.55	2
TOTAL	146	18	280*	7033	54.94	19

The only man to score a double-hundred against five different countries

Mudassar Nazar

First-class

	Inns.	N.O.	H.S.	Runs	Average	100
	336	32	241	13540	44.53	41

Test cricket

v. Australia	30	2	95	893	31.89	–
v. England	26	1	124	858	34.32	3
v. India	25	2	231	1431	62.21	6
v. New Zealand	13	1	106	354	29.50	1
v. Sri Lanka	10	2	81	383	47.87	–
v. West Indies	10	–	41	184	18.40	–
TOTAL	114	8	231	4103	38.70	10

R. G. Pollock

First-class

	Inns.	N.O.	H.S.	Runs	Average	100
	437	54	274	20940	54.67	64

Test cricket

v. Australia	23	2	274	1453	69.19	5
v. England	16	2	137	750	53.57	2
v. New Zealand	2	–	30	53	26.50	–
TOTAL	41	4	274	2256	60.97	7

I. V. A. Richards

First-class

	Inns.	N.O.	H.S.	Runs	Average	100
	656	43	322	30591	49.90	98

Test cricket

v. Australia	46	2	208	2092	47.54	5
v. England	37	3	291	2352	69.17	8
v. India	36	3	192*	1792	54.30	7
v. New Zealand	10	1	105	387	43.00	1
v. Pakistan	27	1	123	1091	41.96	2
TOTAL	156	10	291	7714	52.83	23

Note: By 8 February 1989, Richards had scored 101 centuries

D. B. Vengsarkar

First-class

	Inns.	N.O.	H.S.	Runs	Average	100
	317	42	210	14270	51.89	45

Test cricket

v. Australia	29	4	164*	1146	45.84	2
v. England	38	6	157	1431	44.71	5
v. New Zealand	15	1	75	393	28.07	–
v. Pakistan	35	6	146*	1284	44.27	2
v. Sri Lanka	11	1	166	648	64.80	2
v. West Indies	34	4	159	1486	49.56	6
TOTAL	162	22	166	6388	45.62	17

J. G. Wright

First-class

	Inns.	N.O.	H.S.	Runs	Average	100
	546	37	192	20849	40.96	47

Test cricket

v. Australia	26	1	141	850	34.00	1
v. England	32	2	130	1083	36.10	3
v. India	11	1	110	429	42.90	1
v. Pakistan	15	–	107	512	34.13	1
v. Sri Lanka	7	–	48	162	23.14	–
v. West Indies	18	–	138	535	29.72	1
TOTAL	109	4	141	3571	34.00	7